A SPECIAL
KIND OF
BELONGING

THE CHRISTIAN COMMUNITY

A SPECIAL KIND OF BELONGING

Herbert Wagemaker, Jr., M.D.

WORD BOOKS
PUBLISHER
WACO, TEXAS

A SPECIAL KIND OF BELONGING

Scripture quotation marked KJV is from the King James, or Authorized Version of the Bible. All other quotations are from *The New Testament in Modern English* (Revised Edition) by J. B. Phillips, © J. B. Phillips 1958, 1960, 1972.

ISBN: 0-8499-0072-7
Library of Congress Catalog Card Number: 77-92473
Printed in the United States of America

To Bob and Mary Lou Letsinger—
God's special people in our lives

CONTENTS

1.

COMMUNITY—
A BEGINNING

COMMUNITY—
A BEGINNING

My name blared out on the hospital paging system. I hurried to the phone to see what was going on. Each of my patients flashed through my mind as I dialed the operator. What had gone wrong? Was anyone in trouble?

But this time it had nothing to do with patients. Someone was downstairs in the lobby to see me. With a sigh of relief, I headed for the stairs. In the lobby stood a man with a big smile and dancing eyes—I liked him even before he spoke. I had the feeling there was more to this encounter than mere chance. Bob introduced himself as the new staff man for Intervarsity Christian Fellowship in the area. He and his wife, Mary Lou, had just moved into town and heard about us through some friends. They wanted to meet us.

We went for a cup of coffee. And as I walked back to the hospital after saying goodbye, my heart sang. Here was someone I could really relate to! We had talked that day about his involvement with college students and his excitement about moving to the Gainesville, Florida, area; the University of Florida was a big place with many opportunities, Bob was also looking forward to his involvement with students at nearby Florida State University. His warmth and enthusiasm were contagious; I couldn't wait to get home that night to share the good news with Mary Ann, my wife.

Later on the four of us got acquainted. I found Mary Lou as delightful as Bob. We talked into the night about high school and college kids and how to reach them. We shared our concern for the follow-up work of discipling young Christians. I had been active in Young Life, and was eager to learn from Bob about this, for he had a lot of experience working with young people. That night we prayed together for the kids we would be working with at the University and the high school. We said goodbye with the promise that we would be back together soon. The basis of a good relationship was forming.

As summer turned to fall we saw each other on a more regular basis. We shared our activities, the kids we knew. We prayed for each other and for the people we came in contact with—the more people we met, the more we prayed. We soon learned that involvement with people meant involvement with their problems and struggles, and we talked these over:

"John is in the process of flunking out of school. He has a hard time bringing together his new faith in Christ and what he's learning at the University. He's spinning his wheels and wasting a lot of time."

"A couple met me in my office today to say goodbye. They were on their way to Georgia to get married. I spent over an hour with them and managed to talk them out of going."

A community of shared lives was springing up between us. This new experience of sharing helped us live our lives with more joy and fulfillment. It was a time of discovery, of growing. It was great for me to realize I wasn't alone, that others shared my ideas, my excitement, and my dreams. I was beginning to know more support and love than I ever had!

There were other discoveries as we continued to grow

as a corporate body. We shared the frustrations that we were experiencing as part of our responsibility to one another. We were different! And the differences often led to confrontation:

"You do too much; your life is one mass of activity. You neglect your family and your wife. You're destroying yourself and them in the process."

"If I had to wait on you to get anything in motion, I'd be too old to do anything about it."

"I get sick and tired of your hitting me over the head with the Bible. You're so rigid, uptight and set in your ways. You always pull in God to back up your arguments."

The conflicts were real, and we struggled with them. But the important thing was that we were beginning to deal with areas we generally left to fester by taking the paths of least resistance in our interactions with one another.

As we spent time together we noticed that each of us had some very special, God-given gifts. Bob was very good at laying the foundation for work that would result in college students not only trusting Christ, but continuing to grow and develop into His disciples. Many of his former students are still very active in sharing Christ with others. Mary Lou had the capacity to relate to people on a person-to-person basis, with a love and understanding that helped many people through difficult situations. It soon became obvious that Mary Ann had the gift of relating to the young girls in her camp cabin in such a way that many became Christians. She also stuck with them after that through the struggle of growth and development.

This was a time of great discovery for us. As we learned to share our lives, our relationship became deeper. Not

13

only did we learn things about each other, but we learned things about ourselves. I had to admit my life was a mess of activities and my wife and kids were neglected. I had to rethink some things and come up with some different priorities. I discovered I had a gift for communicating and for teaching.

As time went on, others were invited into the group. Many of our friends were hungry for community; they wanted to get involved in the study of the Bible, the prayers, the sharing. They were allowed to be part of it; we were eager to share some of our discoveries with them. Before we knew it our community became very large; what once had been a group of four came to number twenty and then thirty. There was danger in this, because although we managed to bring along some of the good things into the larger group, the depth of sharing and personal concern was not as great. It couldn't be.

For the four of us the relationship remained very special and unique. We worked together and helped each other. This was a time when we shared each other's ministries and visions. We were involved in each other's growth and development, not only as Christians but as human beings. Even today, after all this time and now at a great distance, we still share in this relationship. When we get together, community is there. Christ's spirit is there. The process of growth and development goes on because of the close, intense community we were part of. It was far from perfect; at times it was frustrating and hard. For all of us, though, it was a time of growing and stretching. It was a time when we felt the excitement and joy of God's new order being part of our lives. It was an introduction to a concept that continues to be a determining force in our lives—the concept of community.

2.

THE CALL TO COMMUNITY

THE CALL TO
COMMUNITY

If we could define a Christian community, we would say it is a group of people who are drawn together around the risen Lord, his teachings, and the Holy Spirit. This community worships together, prays together, and celebrates communion together. Its members share their lives with one another and meet whatever needs are present —spiritual, material, psychological. They spend time together. The community also calls its members into accountability for their actions, their theology, their lives. These people struggle with the idea of relating their Christianity to their lives and to the surrounding community. They also celebrate with joy and love the good things the Lord has provided for them.

This is what the early church was like. During his ministry Jesus called together a group of men from many walks of life. The disciples represented a cross section of their society—Peter and Andrew were fishermen, Simon was a Zealot or superpatriot, Matthew was a tax collector. For three years Jesus lived with these men, attempting to mold them into a community of love. For them it was three years of learning, misunderstanding, and confusion.

Even at Jesus' death this cloud of incomprehension clung to them. Yet after the Resurrection and the coming of the Holy Spirit, these men became the nucleus of

17

the first Christian community. Acts 2 describes what this community was like:

> Everyone felt a deep sense of awe, while many miracles and signs took place through the apostles. All the believers joined together and shared everything in common; they sold their possessions and goods and divided the proceeds among the fellowship according to individual need. Day after day they met by common consent in the Temple; they broke bread together in their homes, sharing meals with simple joy. They praised God continually and all the people respected them. Every day the Lord increased the number of those who were finding salvation (vv. 43–47).

This community was Christ's new order, involved with all aspects of fellowship. The members got together and did many things as a group. (I am sure this included gathering for a good time!) They shared meals in their homes. These people were united in Christ; they were friends!

The fellowship included instruction in the teachings and life of Jesus. Members of the community listened to what the disciples had to say about him out of the experience of living with him. They talked about their beliefs.

There was sharing. People brought together what they had and gave it out as anyone had need. Can you imagine the problems that could cause? What about greedy people? I am sure there was some confronting going on when that happened. The community must have called its members into accountability over these and other matters.

The community was an involved one. The members knew one another. A natural outgrowth of sharing needs and knowing each other would be praying together. The community praised God and gathered in the Temple; day after day Christ's followers worshiped together.

The Christian community was just coming into being. I think we have a tendency to idealize that church, to make it something it wasn't. By doing this, we put it "up there" on a pedestal where we can't reach it. Even a superficial reading of the New Testament should bring us face to face with the fact that these were human beings like we are, with faults and imperfections as well as good qualities. The early church struggled, grew, developed, went backwards, faltered, and struggled some more.

But there was something special about this first Christian community, something that was noticeable to the people around them. The scripture says "all the people respected them." I suspect their way of life formed such a contrast to everything that was around at that time that all who came in contact with the Christians held them in high esteem. It was obvious these people had found a way of life that was real and viable. What they had was attractive. It was vital and vibrant. It had substance and meaning. It drew people into the community, even in the face of imprisonment or death. And even if outsiders didn't believe in the risen Lord, they respected the people who did. They could see the Christians had something; it was evident in their lives.

> Then those who welcomed this message were baptised and on that day alone about three thousand souls were added to the number of disciples. They continued steadily learning the teachings of the apostles, and joined in their fellowship in the breaking of bread and in prayer (Acts 2:41–42).

This is often not the picture in churches today:

"We just don't believe this any more. Christmas and Easter have no historical significance. That's impossible to believe." These words were spoken at the end of a six-week Sunday School series on the validity of Christianity. And the person who spoke was not alone in his thinking. It was the predominant viewpoint in this class of forty young people in a major denominational church. These were attractive, bright church members who couldn't accept the basic presuppositions of the Christian faith. Most of them were closed to the possibility of Christian claims being true. They came to church to see their friends; they wanted their children brought up in the church. But they didn't belong to the body of Christ. They were part of the institution but not the body of believers. This cuts the heart and power out of the body. This removes the reason for the body's existence, the basis for fellowship, the power needed for survival—it reduces the church to an institution like any other.

What a contrast to the vital church of Acts! In two thousand years something has happened. What's gone wrong?

I believe in many instances the church has failed to define the message of the gospel. Church membership has been made a very simple matter with no or very few demands—something that happens almost automatically when a child reaches the proper age. The basic tenets of the gospel remain undefined and amorphous. And it's important that people know what they are committing their lives to.

Some churches have gone too far in the opposite direction. These churches have carefully defined the gospel, made clear the demands of church membership. But they have made the gospel too simplistic. Defining the gospel is a very difficult task; many things are not clear in the scriptures. It's easy to say that God loves the world and came to live with us in human form as Jesus Christ, that he died on a cross to redeem us, rose again, and that now his Holy Spirit is with us. How one interprets this is another thing. How one incorporates this in his or her life is still another. Although the thrust of the gospel is simple, its ramifications can be very complicated. Churches which define the gospel and also define its ramifications in a person's life deprive the person of any freedom. They tie everything up in a neat little package with all the answers and little room for the individual to breathe.

People must know what they are committed to. But it's important that this not be simplistically defined. To protect against this danger, the community must be continually open to reevaluation and redefinition. The scripture must be studied and restudied as a source of information and illumination about the gospel and all it entails.

The failure to define the gospel or the problem of defining it too simplistically are not the only things that keep many churches today from following the model of the community in Acts. Most churches I have contact with are just not set up for the kind of sharing and close fellowship that is necessary. The larger a group grows, the more difficult it becomes to share our lives on a personal basis. Often we don't even know many of our fellow church members; we see them Sunday mornings, perhaps Sunday evenings or at a midweek service, but that's all. We may chat over coffee or while going out the door, but we have very few real opportunities to share what is going on in our lives. As a result, the Christian community lies undiscovered, dormant—and many basic needs go unmet.

This was a problem for me at one time in my Christian life. I struggled with anxieties, feelings of dissatisfaction and incompleteness, and I felt that few of my Christian friends really knew me. I was alone in my walk with the

Lord, or at least felt I was. I couldn't share my doubts about my faith or the teachings of the church; these were written off as spiritual problems and I was advised to deal with them on that level.

My overwhelming need was for a sense that I was not alone in the Lord; I needed a forum to share my life—my whole life—with other Christians. I continued to struggle with these feelings until I stumbled onto the concept of Christian community. This is not unique to me—others had made this discovery long before I did. But although the concept has been with us since Jesus molded the disciples around such an interaction, churches and individuals by and large have failed to grasp so basic an idea.

Now this is not to say that churches must be abolished! It is important for God's people to come together to participate in the Sacraments. There is a need for corporate worship. It is important to be involved in the church as we know it today. But we must incorporate into the existing church structure the opportunity for a sharing fellowship. God's people must know themselves and each other if the Body of Christ is to function.

A way to establish sharing fellowship within the church —one which has made a great difference in my life—is the formation of smaller groups within the church. These groups would consist of eight to twelve people who would meet together frequently to share their lives, to help each other grow and develop in the Christian faith and experience. A sharing group is a place where each member would feel at home, would feel known and cared for. This is the kind of group that grew out of the relationship with Bob and Mary Lou. Now, many years later, I am involved in another such group. It is in these small sharing communities that I have learned most of what I know about the concept of Christian community.

Through small sharing groups such as these the vitality of the church can be recaptured. There can be a fellowship. People can feel they are partakers of a dynamic process, and this in turn can bring new life to our churches and provide those outside the church with a viable option to their present lifestyles.

Now in some places this is going to be impossible. Some churches are just not ready for this. Sharing groups should be started anyway, as outpockets of the church. Christians need to be involved in the activities of the church, and they also need to share their lives in Christian fellowship. Even if this is opposed or resisted it is still a part of what Christ intended for his Body.

The call to the discovery of Christian community starts with the realization that there is one. That's simple enough, but most of us don't even realize it's there. The scripture is filled with concepts about Christian community. We've not discovered these resources yet. We need to look, to read, to study, to discover.

Christian community can take on many forms of sharing. It can be two people who meet regularly to pray and share. It can be a group of people who get together once a week in someone's home. For some, it will mean a very intense encounter in which the group is given a lot of authority over important decisions in people's lives. For others, it means living together in a commune.

I can't define the how of this for anyone. I do know what has been true for me: If I am to grow and develop as a Christian, if I am ever going to experience the real freedom that I know is found in God's "good news," I must be involved in a sharing Christian community that is also a part of the church. Not to be involved would be a denial of my own needs. But there is more to the concept of community than feeling. We are called into a life

23

of sharing by the scriptures, by Christ's teaching and by the example of his early church. Jesus calls us into community. Will we listen to him, hear what he says, and obey him?

3.

A PLACE
WHERE WE
BELONG

A PLACE WHERE
WE BELONG

School was a real struggle for John. In his third year
in college, already six weeks into the fall semester, he was
still having trouble deciding what he wanted to do. He
could never make up his mind what direction to take: "I
start out with real enthusiasm. This always happens at the
beginning. I make a choice. Then, as time goes on, I feel
uncertain that the choice is right. I'm not sure I'll fit into
the spot I've chosen. It seems I'm always looking for a
spot or a place, but never quite find it."

John was feeling the restlessness and anxiety that goes
with not being able to find a place for oneself. We all
need a place to belong, a place where we can feel "at
home."

Paul Tournier discusses this subject in his book, *A
Place for You*. He says there are two worlds—an impersonal world and a world of persons. "This is not so much
a world of men and things, as an impersonal view of
both men and things. The difference is that in the personal
realm, we can and do enter into communication." The
places we're looking for are personal places, places where
we can communicate—where we can belong.

If we are lucky, we experience this kind of belonging
in our family situation. The family is the ideal situation
for learning about the world of the personal; once the

27

sense of belonging has been known, it is easier to rediscover.

But we spend a great part of our lives in the world of the impersonal. Our identities are caught up with who or what we think our place is—with organizations, jobs, professions, clubs. Our friends know us by our associations—"He teaches Sunday School at the Community Church. He practices medicine at Alachua General Hospital." We're identified by our skin color, by what side of town we live on. What does this have to do with the world of the personal? To be sure, there are personal aspects to these things, but if we find our identity in these only, our lives will be robbed of the possibility of real identity, of real belonging.

The Bible makes it clear that as Christians we are pilgrims and strangers in a foreign land, that our home is not here. We don't belong in this world; we are not to conform to it. If this is true, our identity is somewhere other than the world of clubs and professions. But where is it? Must I wait until I get to heaven to find my place? If so, I'm destined to live my life here without identity, without belonging, never feeling at home.

It is interesting that the verb for salvation used in the New Testament has a past, present, and future aspect. The kingdom of God was present back when Jesus was on earth in bodily form. It is here now and it will be present in its perfect form when Christ comes again. If the kingdom is here now, we don't have to wait for the future perfect form (heaven) to be part of it. Our identity is here . . . in the kingdom . . . in the community of Christians.

Jesus was involved in the world he lived in. He mingled with people with whom I would have felt uncomfortable —prostitutes and criminals. He dealt with them on a personal basis. And he calls us to do the same; we are to be salt and light to the world, preservers and illuminators. We are called to be involved in the world we live in—to be personal in an impersonal world.

We can do this because the Christian community is our place to belong. We live in the world, we're part of it, but our true sense of belonging comes from the fellowship of believers. I can reject membership in the American Medical Society. I can lay aside my identity with my service clubs. I can even drop my identity as an Episcopalian. I can let go of my racial identity, my sex role—my ego doesn't tumble if a black man moves into my neighborhood or my wife beats me in tennis. My ego isn't all that involved if I "belong" somewhere else. By being a part of the kingdom, of a community of believers, Christians are freer to walk across the barriers from the impersonal to the personal.

If we find our real identity in the Christian community, we are free to be God's persons in the world. I remember once standing to recite the Pledge of Allegiance in a service club I belong to, and being really bothered by the hypocrisy of saying "with liberty and justice for all." I knew at that moment a large percentage of our people were not receiving justice. I knew that the doors of our club were closed to blacks. But I kept my mouth shut; part of my identity was wrapped up in that club and in what my fellow members thought of me.

Keith Miller, in his book, *The Becomers*, says that the Christian of tomorrow must be both a prophet and a lover. This has been an either/or situation too long. The prophet leaves everyone so angered and embittered that his words are ineffectual; the lover lacks the confrontiveness that helps people see and recognize evil. To cross the line from the impersonal to the personal, one must be both.

29

But this is difficult to do if our identities are caught up in the world. This is what was happening at my club meeting. What was at stake was my identity—where I belong; my concern was with what I could lose if I shot my mouth off. I couldn't afford to be both prophet and lover. The only way I can approach this ideal is if I find my identity in the kingdom of God, in the community of Christians.

Being personal in the world can be painful; being prophet and lover can be risky. Being involved in the world means being open, and being open means risking rejection. I once knew a man who was really hurting, obviously in need of love and support. A group of us took on the challenge of sticking with this man and trying to help him. As time passed he was confronted by things he didn't want to admit, and finally, after much concern, care, and emotional drain, he rejected us. This was hard to accept. We had put ourselves out for this man and his family and he turned his back on us.

This happens. The natural impulse is to not let it happen again. The natural feeling is to pull back, avoid investing in people, to be more calculative. The temptation is to retreat into the impersonal world.

But if we have our identity in the personal kingdom of God, we can risk being personal in the world. We have a home to come to, to have our wounds bound and our needs met. The members of the Christian community are prophets and lovers to one another—confrontative and supportive; it is the Christian community that enables the Christian to be prophet and lover to the world. The community is a place to come back to, a place where we can find our true identity, a place—in the here and now— where we can belong.

4.

DISCOVERING OURSELVES

DISCOVERING
OURSELVES

The Christian community provides a place for us to belong. By doing this, it helps us to discover ourselves. It is one of the few places we will allow ourselves to be seen; therefore it "sees" us as no one else can. It is the one place we can even dare to be real. And because I let myself be known there, my brothers and sisters see me in a way no one else can.

We sometimes videotape families in psychotherapy. When people see how they relate to others, they gain insight into their problems with interpersonal relationships. This is what happens in community. We can't see ourselves very well. But others can. They pick up things we could never see and play them back to us. As a result we learn more about ourselves . . .

What a week it had been! The Inpatient Psychiatric Unit was in complete turmoil. There was a gigantic power struggle going on, and I was caught in the middle of it. I was trying desperately to play it cool and not rock the boat; to survive the residency program I had to get through four months of work in this unit. While I was relating what was going on to my sharing community, someone commented, "you look and sound angry." Yes, I was angry, but that was the first time I had even realized it. I had hidden it from myself to avoid lashing out at the

33

hospital and getting myself in trouble. But it was obvious to everyone else—my community, my family, surely the staff and patients. For me it was a great discovery, the first step toward coming to grips with the situation. During that evening I discovered that I could trust my community with my anger. They didn't reject me because of it; as a matter of fact, they helped me admit it and deal with it.

Finding out I was full of anger was a new experience for me—a discovery. There still is anger in me. But I'm more in touch with it now than ever before, and this helps me handle my anger better.

Sometimes it's easier to discover the negative aspects of ourselves than it is to find out the good ones. The sharing community also helps its members discover their gifts and talents and then perfect them and use them.

Several years ago, if someone had asked me, "What are your gifts?" I would probably have answered, "Well, let's see . . . I can play the harmonica, and the thumb on my right hand is double-jointed." As a matter of fact, I didn't know what my gifts were. I didn't even think about gifts even though I knew we were supposed to have them.

In the twelfth chapter of 1 Corinthians, Paul writes at great length about gifts. He compares the Christian community to the human body, made up of many different parts functioning together. A basketball player can grab a pass out of midair, jump up, measure the distance between his hand and the basket and push the ball toward the basket before his feet hit the floor again. The eyes are involved in this. So is the brain. Messages are sent to the muscles in the legs and feet, the hands and arms, so that just the right amount of push is put behind the ball to get it into the basket. This is an example of the unity and coordination Paul was talking about in 1 Corinthians.

If the parts don't function together, the ball can't even make it to the basket, let alone go through it.

The Christian community is like the human body. It has parts—you and me and many others. Somehow, it has to work together to accomplish God's task here on earth. The big problem is that many of us don't even realize that God has given us very special, unique gifts. They remain hidden and dormant.

Not long ago, while going through some stuff of mine at my parents' house, I found a birthday card my grandmother had sent me over twenty years ago. Inside the card was five dollars. All these years the gift had remained hidden and dormant. Now I rejoiced in the fact that her thoughtfulness was made apparent to me.

I'm like this when it comes to God's gifts. Even after I learned that he has given *everyone* gifts, I had a hard time believing that applied to me. Once, after I had given a speech, someone came up to me and said, "you have a real gift for communicating." I thought to myself, "That's a gift?"; I had been so nervous before I spoke that I couldn't eat my supper; my stomach had been tied up in knots. Other times when I would be told I had gifts, I would say, "No, it's nothing, it really doesn't amount to much." I would put down the very gifts I had, rather than using them to the fullest.

As we grow more in touch with ourselves within the Christian community, we reveal more of ourselves to our brothers and sisters. They help us discover and develop our gifts and talents. They provide the climate of trust that lets us dare to show ourselves, to say, "I'd really like to try teaching a Sunday School class but I'm scared." Or, "I'd like to lead a small group but I feel it would fail." Within the climate of love and acceptance we can try, we can discover, we can grow and stretch out.

Several people had graduated from college and moved away from our leadership community, leaving some empty positions to be filled. The community got together one night and prayed about this situation. And that night several things happened. A few young people were picked to fill the positions. These people were picked because of the gifts the community saw in them, and for their spiritual maturity. I remember that night well. It was as if the community was calling these people out for a special mission under the guidance of the Holy Spirit. The community recognized the gifts, affirmed them, and commissioned the people who had them.

That was more dramatic than usual. Sometimes, gifts are discovered just by trying something new. Two members of our couples group were asked to head a Faith-Alive mission that involved church renewal at our church. They were rather reluctant to do this, and brought it up one night at our meeting. They couldn't see themselves doing this sort of thing, but the community felt they had the gifts for it. They were affirmed and encouraged in the task and did a fine job. Without the community they probably wouldn't even have tried it.

Paul had several interesting lists of gifts mentioned in the scriptures. The list in 1 Corinthians includes messengers, preachers, teachers, workers of spiritual powers, healing, helpers, organizers and people who speak in tongues. I am quite sure these lists are incomplete. We get sidetracked if we think that any one of these gifts is more important than the others. Again and again, Paul counters this type of thinking by saying *all* the gifts of God are important. Christ's Body needs them all.

We come to our communities as unique people. Each has a biological makeup different from anyone else in the world. We've also had different social experiences. We've all received different gifts from the Lord. How then can we look, think, and sound the same? People need to be involved in the exciting business of discovering how best to use their unique personalities. This happens in a setting where they're allowed to be themselves, where they're not forced, pushed, or molded. "I found out that I could really share my faith with a friend at work. Wow! I never thought I could." It is exciting to see someone else discover his or her gifts and put them to use.

Another thing the community does is help us hear and discover God's will for our personal lives. These people know and love us, and desire that we find and follow God's will:

"I want you to pray with me tonight that God will reveal his will to us about taking this new job."

"I feel that with your gifts and abilities, this new job was made for you."

"I've felt for a long time now that you have had a real restlessness over your job situation. Perhaps this is God's way of leading you into a new one."

"I've also sensed uneasiness in you over the past few months. I know you are not happy in your work. This could be God's answer for you."

When we struggle with finding God's direction in our lives and share this with the community, they become ears for us. Together we try to find God's will. We talk together, pray together, and listen together. The community has given me real insight into the mind of God. This has come through the scriptures, praying, and listening to his voice through his people. He speaks to them in a way I can hear, a way that gets through to me.

The process of discovering ourselves and others in the sharing community is a slow one. We all have a great drive to know and be known by others. At the same time we fear being known; we keep people away. But I know a lot more about myself than I once knew. I've discovered some of my gifts, perfected them, and used them. I've discovered areas in my life that need changing, and I'm working on those. I've learned to know other people in a way that was impossible before—seeing things from their point of view, looking at things in different ways. I hope the Christian community will continue to be this type of place for me. We all need discovery in our lives—the community of brothers and sisters provides this for me.

5.

WHOLENESS AND HEALING

WHOLENESS AND HEALING

God intended for all of us to have abundant lives, to be persons involved in the process of wholeness. The Christian community, with the work of the indwelling Holy Spirit, helps us become that type of person.

Psychology, over the past few decades, has been blessed with some thinkers who are very humanistically oriented; that is, they are very interested in helping human beings grow and develop. The humanistic psychologists talk about man's uniqueness and worth. And although there are points of difference, they have much to say to Christians, for we believe that God created us as individuals, each with unique gifts and talents to be used in special ways for his purposes.

Out of the thinking of these humanistic psychologists has grown the human potential movement with its chief spokesman, A. H. Maslow. Dr. Maslow, in his book, *The Farther Reaches of Human Nature*, states that man is a creative being and that we should strive to be creative. Maslow feels that the experts, not the average man, should determine what is normal. If we want to understand art, for example, we go to an artist, not the average man on the street; we try to learn how he perceives art and to copy him.

Maslow calls the creative person a self-actualizing person. This is a man who is in touch with himself, his feelings, his emotions, his thoughts, his impulses. He has discovered his talents and gifts and is perfecting them. He is in the process of growing and developing to his maximum capabilities.

Maslow made a study of people he considered self-actualizing and listed their common characteristics. These people have high callings that come from without, in the priestly sense. They are selfless in the sense that they forget themselves and get involved without thought of failure or what will happen. They're not timid; they're into things "whole hog." They're people who make small choices for wholeness many times during the day. They move away from security and dependency into new areas. They do things that will expose, rather than hide, them.

Self-actualizing people are in tune with themselves. They know what they like and why, and they aren't afraid to express their likes and dislikes. Red Skelton once said about a picture, "I don't like it and I don't care who does; I don't." Self-actualized people are like that; they know how they feel.

Self-actualized people also don't play games or hedge. When they doubt, they are honest about it. They take responsibility for themselves and their decisions or actions; they don't blame others for their state of affairs. They are people who dare to be different, to be unique, to be unpopular. They ignore fear.

Finally, self-actualized people are in process. They have not yet arrived, and they know it. They are still working on their potential—continuously finding out who they are, where they are going, what is good or bad for them. They listen to their own voices, work hard, keep on growing and seeking their mission in life.

The self-actualized person is what God created us to

be. We have different talents and gifts; we are creative—wholeness has to do with discovering this and living it out in our lives.

What we're really saying is that wholeness is a whole process of growth and development, of changing, of moving, of becoming all we can be. To initiate this process, we must realize the necessity of change. We must look at things from different points of view, evaluate ourselves and be willing to expose things that shouldn't be there. The sharing community is a perfect place for this to happen; the community should be a place where whole persons are made.

There's a real difference between wholeness and healing. Wholeness involves the process of what we're becoming. Healing is a process that has to do with what's gone on in the past. These things, of course, go together, but healing needs to happen before wholeness can really progress. Many times the things we need to be healed from hinder the process of wholeness; they hold us back.

We are all in need of healing. We have hurts that go back a long way in our lives. We also have daily hurts that need to be healed. A group acts as a healing community when it ministers to hurting people. Members of the group become the healers by listening, being concerned, and showing love:

"Last night I asked my son to leave the house. We just couldn't put up with him any more. Today, I feel shattered; it's like the world has stopped for me." As Tom told his story the group listened intently. Concern was written on every face there. One could feel the group reach out in love for Tom, providing the setting for healing to take place.

"Maybe you can get together with your son, sit down, and talk it over. It's important that you don't drive him away from you." Words were also used to convey love and concern to Tom. And he listened, because he knew these people cared about him and his relationship with his son. The love he felt in the group started him on the road to healing.

Healing sometimes takes place when people are forced out of their old patterns of relating. This was the case with Helen. Helen couldn't stand confrontation; she would run from the room, shattered, when arguments within the group became heated. And she would do almost anything to avoid confrontation herself. This pattern of relating was affecting all her relationships. She let her husband dominate her, but she fought back by undermining him—he would make plans to go somewhere she didn't want to go and she, rather than confronting him directly, would simply not be ready on time. They fought—he in a direct, dominating way and she very sweetly, helplessly, and effectively.

The group recognized that Helen's pattern of avoiding confrontation was destructive. They then attempted to make Helen see this. Often a person will do almost anything to avoid seeing that they're relating badly; the process of bringing it to their attention requires time, patience, love, and understanding.

Helen's maid was taking advantage of her. She was always late, not doing her work, and making Helen angry. Once Helen had been made to see the problems with her pattern of behavior, the group insisted that she change it. They were loving but firm; they demanded that she confront her own mind:

"I can't help it; I feel so resentful. My maid is really taking advantage of me, and I can't do anything about it. I feel helpless."

"You've got to confront her and tell her. Look what

this is doing to you; you're angry and resentful. You've got to do this."

With the help of the group, Helen began to be healed of her destructive pattern of relating. She learned that she didn't have to put up with the anger and resentment that went with being walked on. She grew stronger; as time went on she was able to tolerate the heated confrontations that sometimes took place in the group. And she began to assert herself with her husband, to say "No, I don't want to do it that way" rather than undermining his decisions. She began to see that she was a person with ideas and thoughts, likes and dislikes, and that confrontation could strengthen rather than destroy her personhood. As she learned new patterns of relating she was on the road toward becoming a whole, self-actualized person.

And she was discovering the healing qualities within herself, learning to use and develop them. One night during another group meeting, Jo Ann was confronted and couldn't stand it. She left the room. It was Helen who followed her, who listened to her, who showed her love and understanding and support. That night healing came to Jo Ann in the form of Helen.

This is what happens in the sharing community—the Christian community is a healing community. The members learn to listen, to show concern, to be firm when needed and understanding when necessary. We're all part of the process of healing and being healed.

6.

THE PROCESS
OF LIBERATION

THE PROCESS OF
LIBERATION

The other day at the hospital I walked through the newborn nursery. The babies there were pink, vibrant, alive—already intensely involved in the life process. A little later, walking down the street, I noticed the faces of people as they walked past me. What a contrast! The faces I saw were sad, dull, expressionless—hardly alive.

What, besides fifty years or so, had happened between the nursery and the street? Something surely had gone wrong. What I saw on the street were constricted, lifeless people. This is what I see in my psychiatric practice. Many of my friends are like this also. Even worse, that's the way I am, more than I want to admit. So many of us are "uptight"—lifeless, unable to relax, unable to feel or think freely.

Fred was in his late forties—a successful corporation lawyer, one of the leading attorneys in his firm. For all intents and purposes Fred had "made it." But he came to see me very depressed and disillusioned; he felt his life had suddenly turned sour. As I worked with Fred, I found he was a very compulsive person. He got up at the same time every day, got to work earlier than everyone else, followed a strict schedule. At work he was always very businesslike, with no time for laughter or any of the little things that make a working situation pleasant. Fred was the same way at home—things were done in order, at the proper time. Family relationships were very formal; the wife and kids never broke the pattern. There was no room in Fred's life for spontaneity. Now the pattern was breaking down and he was feeling the pangs of this as depression. Fred's was a drastic form of uptightness.

Sally was uptight too, although not as seriously as Fred. She smiled as we talked in my office, but her eyes flashed. "John brought home three people from the office the other night, even though he knew I had plans to go out that evening. He expected me to drop everything and fix supper." When asked how she felt about that, she said, "Well, I was hurt, but in the end I was happy that I could be a submissive wife." Pressed a little further, she admitted, "Well, I was a little angry also." It was obvious that Sally was more than a little angry; it was written all over her face. She looked mad and acted mad. But she wasn't aware of it; she had shoved it into her subconscious mind and gotten it out of the way. But her denial of her anger was blunting all her emotions; she had trouble feeling love and joy as well as anger.

Last night on the tennis court, I was so uptight I either hit everything out or into the net. Maybe it was the fear of getting beat or just the end of a bad day, but I just didn't have the freedom to swing naturally. We all have our moments of uptightness. The opposite of this is what we're created to be—free. We want freedom. Then why are we so uptight?

To understand the mechanisms of uptightness, we need to look at some basic concepts of the mind formalized by Sigmund Freud and others. I don't want to imply that Freud was Christian or that we must accept everything he says. But he did have great insight into the workings of the mind, and we can learn from him.

Think of the mind as an iceberg. We know that only about one-tenth of that massive piece of ice is above water. Very similarly, one-tenth of our minds is in the conscious realm. The rest is the unconscious—the underwater part. There are different depths of the unconscious. Some material is stored near the conscious realm, in the preconscious area. We can recall the name of a person we haven't seen or thought of in years; it is filed away in the preconscious area ready for use when we need it. Other material is stored at such great depth it's very difficult to recall. Students of the mind know that this material is available because it can be gotten to through the use of medication—"truth" serum.

We put material in the unconscious areas of our minds for several reasons. Certainly it's an area where we store things for future use. As a matter of fact, every experience, thought, and feeling is stored in our minds, filed away as if the brain were a giant computer.

However, the mind does more than store information. It protects us by placing in the unconscious memories and feelings that would threaten us or make us anxious if they were brought to the surface. For instance, if you were hurt in a serious accident, the pain and fright and anxiety of that experience may be kept from your conscious mind so you won't have to experience it again. Perhaps you feared the dark as a child. The feelings of terror may be pushed into the unconscious so that they don't recur whenever you are in a dark place.

The mind also keeps impulses that generate in the unconscious from breaking into the conscious as parts of our existence. These impulses are the driving forces of our emotional lives; Freud called the originator of these forces the "id." If, for instance, you find yourself in a heated argument, the driving force of your id might say "sock him in the nose." Perhaps you have every right to punch him in the nose. But if you did, and he was bigger or stronger than you are, you would be in real trouble. To protect you in that situation, that thought or impulse never comes into your conscious mind. The set of forces that keeps the original impulse in the unconscious is called the "ego."

Holding all this material in the unconscious recesses of the mind takes energy. These thoughts, feelings, and impulses are all trying to be expressed. When a lot of this type of material is repressed, the ego is deprived of its strength and deprived of the energy that it needs to do other things.

The ego of the uptight person, then, is sapped of its energy. The person who is uptight lacks the energy to look at new ideas, to relate to his friends or his family. There will be little joy or laughter in his life; as a matter of fact, he may be very depressed. This type of person is usually very compulsive and rigid; he's all business. He's tired all the time, yet he can't sleep at night. His neck and head hurt; his face shows no emotion; he looks, acts, and feels older than he is. He's not in tune with himself or anyone else; hence his life has lost its joy and meaning, its creativity.

In order to be freed of an uptight existence, a person needs to get at this material that lies in the unconscious, to release it and let it go. The problem is how. Fred was more uptight than most of us; he needed professional help. In therapy I tried to get at those feelings and impulses in the unconscious and create a safe atmosphere for Fred to release some of that repressed material.

Sally's problem was that she had been trying to cut off what she saw as "bad" emotions. We've been well-conditioned to believe that our impulses are wrong and that we should get rid of them. We forget that they, too, are created by God as an important part of our minds; they signal us when our bodies are in need, and we would die without them. This doesn't mean that we act on every impulse that breaks into our minds—we don't. But we need to acknowledge them; trying to push those impulses into the subconscious, to deny their existence, can have negative effects.

I tried to point out to Sally that anger and other emotions are part of life, that feeling anger did not make her a bad person. Repressing her emotions was having a narrowing effect on her life. Once she realized that it is OK to feel angry, she was able to begin opening up to all her emotions, to partake of life more abundantly.

The sharing community is an ideal forum for the process of being freed from uptightness. It's important that we get in contact with our feelings, thoughts, and impulses. Getting at this material involves the process of sharing in a group where we are loved, supported— where we can feel trust. This doesn't happen all at once but over a period of time. The more we share our thoughts, emotions, and impulses, the more we're able to share. And the more we get in touch with ourselves.

This has happened to me: "I'm really mad. I'm boxed in an impossible situation. I have the responsibility for my patients, but no power to do anything about it. If I could catch so and so outside the hospital, I'd push his face in." I had let my anger out in the open, full force. And my Christian community still loved me. They accepted my anger and took a great weight off my shoulders. With my anger and my violent impulses out in the open, I was freed as a person.

It is as important that we be freed to think our thoughts as to feel our feelings. The Christian community can be involved in this liberating process. Bill was graduating from college. In the past two years he had gone through some real changes; he had dropped out of church and his parents were very concerned. He said, "I'm somewhat confused about God. My friends and some of my professors don't believe in anything. I've tried to talk to my folks about this, but they just said I need more faith and that things would work out. When I was in high school I tried to talk to my pastor, but he told me that I shouldn't doubt, that I should clear my mind of the thoughts I was having."

For Bill this was bad advice. He had pushed those thoughts into his unconscious mind, ignored them, but they had not gone away. Had someone helped him with them earlier, perhaps they would not have become so overwhelming.

Christians have an unhealthy fear of the intellect. This is one reason we repress some of our questions about faith and discourage our children's questions. We seem to fear that delving into these questions will "pull the plug," that if we face our doubts our beliefs will go down the drain. My experience has shown the opposite: our faith and beliefs are strengthened by dealing with our doubts. Difficult problems are never solved by ignoring them or denying their existence, but by looking at them and dealing with them.

In our sharing group we talked things over with Bill. We found that a lot of his problems centered around the need to find reliable answers. He soon learned that everything he had been taught by his professors and everything his friends thought was not necessarily true. If we could do more of this, fewer of our young people would fall away from Christianity during their college years. Most of us have doubts. It's helpful to work through these things as a community where there is love, acceptance, and understanding.

One of the hardest things any of us have to deal with is our own imperfection. I'm a perfectionist; I tend to feel that if I make mistakes I won't be accepted—my friends will reject me, my family will reject me, God will reject me. And I reject myself. This is poor reasoning and terrible theology; it takes grace out of the picture completely. As Christians we know that God forgives our thoughts, feelings, and actions. God accepts us just as we are, faults and all. The Christian community provides the human side of this acceptance.

As a physician, I've had to come to grips with the fact that I've made mistakes in diagnosis and treatment of some of my patients. And I struggle with imperfection in every other aspect of my life. Through the sharing community I have been freed from the need to be perfect. As I have learned about and accepted my own imperfections, I have also become a lot more tolerant of the mistakes of others. I have been enabled to play the liberating role in the lives of others.

The gospel is truly a liberating force, the best release from the constriction of uptightness. As we come to know ourselves, to admit our impulses and emotions, our thoughts and our imperfections to ourselves and others, we are freed to live more abundantly. A sharing community helps in this process.

7.

DEMANDS OF COMMUNITY

DEMANDS OF
COMMUNITY

If our relationships with other human beings are going to be meaningful, they will cost us something. Relationships are demanding. Sometimes after supper I sneak into my bedroom just to be alone—to read or watch television. But if I did this all the time, rather than spending time with my wife and children, I would be hurting my relationship with my family. Family relationships are perhaps more demanding than any other—to have good ones we have to give of ourselves. But the relationships which we develop in the Christian community also make demands of us.

For me a major cost of community is time—it takes another night out of an already impossible schedule. One night a week doesn't seem like much, but as time goes on, it adds up. This is especially true when I'm tired; to come home "beat" and then go to my community group meeting can be very hard on me. My time is also invested in other areas because of the group and the effect it has on my life.

But in community more is demanded of us than our time. We must give of ourselves and reach out to our brothers and sisters where their need is. They do the same for us. Sometimes tragedy occurs, and if one member of the body suffers, we all suffer. The emotional involvement demanded by the community can be draining.

Community demands that we be committed to the uniqueness of each of these people we share our lives with. This is not an easy thing for me, because my natural tendency is to control, to manipulate, and to force. I am committed to the discovery of our gifts together, and to contributing to the atmosphere that allows for this process. It took me a long time to realize God created us to be unique and different, and that our differences make the community better and help us all grow and develop.

Community requires that each of us be committed to the group process and the work of the Holy Spirit through it. The Holy Spirit teaches us through each other and through the community. This means that when the community speaks, we listen; we consider its point of view carefully and usually act accordingly. We relinquish some of our self-direction. Even when we're in conflict with the community, we don't pass off lightly what they say. We come to the group for advice. They're involved in the major decisions and problems of our lives. We give them this power because we believe in the integrity of the process.

A friend in Atlanta told me that in his Christian community the major life decisions, such as moving to another community or taking a new job, are community decisions. Members of the group have turned over to the community the right of choice in these areas. The extent to which the individual gives up his or her decision-making powers differs according to the specific community, but this type of thing goes on in most of the communities I know. And this can be difficult. We live in a world that tells us to make up our own minds; it's hard to release or to share that power. But community demands it.

As I've become more involved in the whole process of community, I've lost some of my individualism. This has been hard for me. To turn over to a group of people some controls that I've had in the past took time and some effort. It still does; my tendency is to reclaim some of the controls I've relinquished. My community isn't really very demanding; it doesn't make major decisions for me like moving or changing jobs. We don't pool our money for community needs. Maybe it should do these things. I need to struggle further in these and other areas regarding the demands of the community.

One of the most difficult demands of community is personal vulnerability. If we are to be involved in community, we have to begin to reveal things about ourselves that we normally hide; some of our masks must come off and expose our inner selves. This can be a painful experience; in letting ourselves be known we risk hurt and rejection. We also risk being shown things about ourselves we would rather ignore; personal vulnerability involves being open to what the group shows us. The community often acts as a mirror and lets us see what kind of person we are. My first reaction to being confronted with things I don't like about myself is to draw back, to defend myself, to deny what the group has brought up to me. But in order to fulfill the purposes of the community, we must keep ourselves open to the group.

Being involved in community demands that we be held accountable for our commitments and the quality of our lives. This doesn't mean that we should be held to a bunch of superficial rules governing what we look like, what we eat and drink, what we can or cannot do. Accountability in community applies to the important areas of how we relate to others, what kind of people we are.

61

We're all different; it is important that we be held accountable for being our own unique selves, not for conforming to a group norm.

Accountability can have very broad ramifications. If I agree to spend time talking to the residents of a nursing home and then let it slip out of my schedule, I must be called into account. If I have been confronted with areas in my life that need working on—perhaps I've wronged someone or neglected my wife and children—I need to be held accountable for making changes. We are all accountable for using the gifts we have discovered. Some people feel that Christian communities should call members into accountability over how they spend their money. For some, Christian community involves living together and sharing everything from possessions to personal decisions.

I have some basic problems with accountability; in many ways, it's just against my nature. I don't want to be held accountable. Now, I can say, "I'm accountable to God; he directs me." That sounds good, but for me that often means, "I'll do it on my own." I don't like others saying, "Look, what about this?" or "We think you have to deal with that." There's enough basic rebellion in me to resist being told what I need to do. But I have found that if I'm really going to change I must be held accountable to my group. I used to think that examinations in school were worthless and should be eliminated. Then I found that I didn't study unless I was tested. I don't change, either, unless I'm called into account.

And change is one of the basic demands, not only of community, but of life itself. This concept of process, of change, permeates the Scripture; in the Bible salvation is seen as a continuous process with a past (the Christ event and our own personal acceptance of its meaning), a present (our present life in Christ), and a future (our continued growth and development as a Christian until the day when we'll be transformed, and therefore suitable for God's ultimate community). Yet Christians as a group seem to resent change and to struggle against it. I know this is true for me. It is much more comfortable to keep the same theology, the same political views, the same lifestyle, and I like my life to be as comfortable as possible. But God doesn't call us to a comfortable existence; he calls us to be his people. And this involves the process of growth and development, of change.

The community demands change and offers a place for this process to take place. By exposing us to many different points of view, it gives us the opportunity for change. And by holding us accountable for being our own best selves, it keeps us in the process of changing even when we would rather stay comfortably stagnant.

Living in community is not easy. The Christian community demands that we make commitments and take risks when we would rather not. Growth in community can be painful and frustrating—certainly uncomfortable. But I believe the process is worthwhile, for it brings us closer to being what we were created to be.

As my sharing group has met and studied God's word, prayed, and shared our lives, each of us has changed. We've all had to look at the priorities in our lives—time is spent in different ways now. My political views are different now than when I first began meeting with the group. I've lost some of my worldly identity. How I relate to people has changed. As I look at the changes in my life, I'm thankful. They represent struggle, growth and development. I'm also well aware of the fact that there's much to do in every area of my life. I'm a long way from where I should be. The struggle goes on, but it's a struggle that adds to life.

8.

THE COMMUNITY OF LOVE

THE COMMUNITY
OF LOVE

It was obvious from the start that Bill had a real problem with alcohol. He usually drank before he came to the group, and occasionally we couldn't even understand what he was saying. Sue was selfish; her whole life centered around herself. When she talked, it was about her wants, wishes and desires. Helen had such a poor self-concept that she never dared confront anyone. She preferred to retreat into her shell and isolate herself from everyone else.

We all bring our problems with us when we join the group. We may try to hide the most obvious ones. But the group process is such that sooner or later they will be exposed and confronted. Opening ourselves in this way can be very risky; confrontation can help a person grow but it can also destroy him. But looking back on the way our community handled these problems, I can't think of a single instance in which members were confronted in a destructive way. The reason for this is love. The Christian community is a loving community, and love plays an important part in the group process.

The kind of love I'm talking about can be tough. It calls us into accountability; it demands that we make changes in our lives. But it tells us in a voice we are ready to hear, one we can understand. Sometimes love can mean ignoring the obvious, at least for a while, when a person doesn't have the strength to be confronted, when facing the truth would destroy him. In the group, confrontation means more than just the truth; confrontation means speaking the truth in love.

Sometimes a person has very destructive forces inside of him. Love helps the community deal with these forces in a person, both when they're turned outward toward others and when they're turned inward toward himself.

This doesn't mean that everything always works perfectly in the group process. Members of the group are human, they're often selfish and sometimes cruel. People can get hurt; they are sometimes confronted when they're not ready to listen. But a general atmosphere of love can make up for poor timing or specific unloving actions.

The love that transforms the group process doesn't originate within the group members; it originates with God. It's difficult to understand this kind of love without experiencing it through Christ and the Holy Spirit. It involves much more than the intellectualization of theological facts or historical events; it involves somehow coming to grips with the significance of the incarnation, the crucifixion, the resurrection. This kind of love comes from internalizing the meaning of Jesus' life and ministry.

I can't get this kind of love merely by thinking about love. It can happen only because the Spirit of God has come into my very being and transformed me. This is what happens to the brothers and sisters in the Christian community—they are filled with God's love. It is present in people who have experienced it and who are content only when this love grows in them and is shared with others. This is the force that's operational in the Christian community, the force that makes change a possibility.

In that first community of Jesus, there was a tax collector named Matthew. Tax collectors were despised by the Jews, especially the superpatriots—the Zealots. There also happened to be in that first group of twelve a Zealot named Simon. When these two men walked arm in arm down the street, calling each other Brother Matthew and Brother Simon, love was visible. And this is the type of love I'm talking about—the transforming love of God. Shouldn't our Christian communities be like this also? *

* Taken from Clarence Jordon.

9.

THE SERVANT COMMUNITY

THE SERVANT
COMMUNITY

Jesus came to serve, "not to be ministered unto, but to minister" (Matt. 20:28, KJV). That was probably the hardest thing the people around Jesus had to learn. They thought he was to be a king who would drive the enemies out of the land and restore it once more. Towards the end of his career on earth Jesus tried to show his disciples the true nature of his mission by a symbolic act; one night after supper he rose from the table, took off his outer clothes, tied a towel around his waist, poured water in a basin, and started to wash the dirt of the streets off his disciples' feet. He had done this to several of the disciples when he came to Simon Peter. What a human response Peter made: "Not me, Lord"! Peter still hadn't grasped what Jesus was trying to tell him. I'm sure that later, after the Resurrection, the disciples discussed that night. I imagine Peter saying, "Remember, I wouldn't let him wash my feet. All the time he was trying to show us that he came to serve."

Because we follow Christ, we too are called to be servants. And the Christian community is a servant community. It is made of people who serve, or at least try to. This involves discovering needs both within and outside the community, and seeing that these needs are met. This can involve group action or the action of individuals

73

who have been nurtured in their lives and faith by living in community.

It goes without saying that we live in a very needy world. There are always poor people who are hungry and homeless. Many of our older people are neglected and lonely and desperate. Many children are in bad home situations, don't receive adequate medical care. Newly-released prisoners have trouble finding jobs and places to stay.

There are broader questions of need. Right now, many people in the world are starving. Do we as Christians have a responsibility to see that something is done about this? People who represent us in our governments need to know how we feel. What do we do when our country only helps those people who share our beliefs and follow our political system? These are complex questions; there will not be agreement within the community or among Christians in general as to their exact implications. But being a servant community requires being aware and concerned about these things.

We don't have to go across the city or across the nation to find need. Families in our own neighborhoods are going through great turmoil. Couples are on the verge of divorce; their children are in all kinds of trouble ranging from school problems to confrontations with the police. People have spiritual and psychological needs. Many are depressed, isolated in their own worlds, living in a constant state of desperation. The Christian community is called to serve in these kinds of situations.

There are times when it's easy for me to serve, when the people I deal with are nice and appreciate what I'm doing and thank me. At these times I feel good for having been a servant. But other times I just don't want to serve. One night I was called to the emergency room at about 2:00 A.M. Old Charlie was there again—drunk and dirty. He smelled of stale booze and looked a mess. It was late; I was tired. Servant? I was in no mood to serve anybody, especially old drunken Charlie. I did the easiest thing I could think of at the moment; I put him in the hospital. Later, when I came back to check on my patients, old Charlie had slept it off and was a little better. I still didn't feel like being a servant—not to him anyway. But we are called to serve the Charlies of the world as well as those whom it's more pleasant to serve.

Serving can take many specific forms. It can mean food or money. It can mean taking people to the doctor, or cleaning their houses for them. Or it may mean just being with a person, supporting him or her during a crisis. How each person and each sharing community works out the concept of his or her own servanthood will be different. We all have different gifts along these lines. As we share ourselves with our community, different ways of serving will show themselves to us.

One of the most important aspects of Christian servanthood is learning to meet needs on a personal level. People are helped most effectively on a one-to-one basis. I talked recently to a woman who was having trouble with her son. She said, "I don't know what to do. John's having problems at school. He's gone from all *A*'s and *B*'s to *C*'s and *D*'s. He doesn't study any more and has been caught several times skipping school. I think he's into all kinds of drugs; the gang he hangs around with has that reputation. It's hard raising a teenage boy without a father around. He's hard for me to control."

John's mother needed some effective help. She had some real problems that needed to be dealt with. But what she needed first of all was to be listened to. There is no way to discover what is going on without listening.

As I listened to this woman, I couldn't help but be concerned for her. I understood her situation and empathized with her. I'm sure she felt this when I listened to her. This is how helping begins—with listening and with empathetic understanding. I wish it began with advice, because I like to give advice. I wish we could start with people's spiritual needs, but in these kinds of situations most people aren't even aware of their spiritual needs. To be truly helpful, to be a true servant, we must begin by trying to tune into a person's immediate needs. Then I can try to meet those needs; in this particular case I brought John and his mother together to enable them to get some things out in the open. This helped; John tried to understand his mother's concern for him, and she tried to see his need for friends. Together they're trying to work things out, and things have changed around their house.

Some people have trouble revealing their needs to another person. Helping them takes time, understanding, and the development of a deeper personal relationship. This was the case with Mary. Mary was quiet, shy, always on the fringe of things. She never really got involved in anything. In talking to her, I found that she had been hurt by some friends of hers. They had told others things which she had shared with them in confidence, and so she was having a hard time trusting anyone. This was Mary's basic problem—trusting people. I could have explained to her that although some people aren't trustworthy, others are. But she didn't need to be told, she needed to experience the fact. I had to be a trustworthy person to her.

What I'm really talking about is sharing our lives with other people. This is the natural outgrowth of being involved in Christian community—by our very nature, as members of God's community, we are interested in other people and their needs. When we're turned on to this great experience in life, we want to involve others in it. We have been helped to overcome our problems, to discover ourselves and become what God wants us to be; naturally we want to help others in this process.

But helping people takes more than just wanting to be a helpful person. Some ways of helping can be more harmful than neglect. Carl Rogers writes about the characteristics of a truly helpful person in his book, *Becoming a Person*. His concepts have proven useful to many; they are worth repeating. According to Rogers, the person who wants to help others should ask himself the following questions:

1) "Can I be the kind of person who will be perceived by the other person as trustworthy, as dependable or consistent in a deep sense?" It is important that we communicate to the person we're dealing with that he can trust and confide in us. This feeling of trustworthiness must usually be built up over a period of time. A willingness to listen conveys trustworthiness. So does being careful to keep confidential what is said to us.

2) "Can I be expressive enough that what I am feeling is communicated unambiguously?" We must be in tune with ourselves so we don't send out signals that are unclear. If, for instance, I am annoyed with one of my patients but put on a calm, tolerant facade, the message that I communicate may be ambiguous and confusing, because the patient will sense the annoyance but not be able to confront it directly. It is safer to avoid hiding feelings from ourselves or the person we are trying to help. This kind of honesty is difficult to maintain; it's never fully realized, but it is very important. People need honest feedback from other human beings.

In a session in my office, a young patient told me, "I can't get up in the mornings; I feel sick and nauseated. I must drop my math course; I'm sure I'll be all right then." I responded, "You're trying to manipulate me into giving you a medical excuse for dropping the course. I just don't feel that what's going on is open and aboveboard." Then we were able to talk about what was happening. Had I not been honest with my feelings, this young man would never have dealt with his manipulative behavior.

3) "Can I myself experience positive attitudes toward this other person—attitudes of warmth, caring, liking, interest, respect?" This isn't always easy. We sometimes shy away from this type of personalness because it makes demands on us and leaves us vulnerable. Caring puts us out on a limb—what happens if we care and invest ourselves and people reject us? Yet caring is necessary for helping people.

We have to recognize the possibility that we may not be able to respond positively to some people, that we may just be unable to feel warm and friendly about them. Perhaps in these instances it would be better to let someone else handle the situation. Can we let this happen, or do we want to "hold on" to people even though we may not be helpful to them? How much ego involvement is there in our servanthood? Who are we helping, them or us?

4) "Can I be a strong enough person to be separate from the other?" Maintaining my integrity, my identity is the only way I can help another person. If I'm manipulated like everyone else, I can hardly be part of a learning experience for anyone; I'm part of the problem. There's a real line of distinction here between sympathy—giving people what they want, and empathy—giving people what they need to grow and develop. We want to be

helpful; we want to give. But helping people doesn't always mean doing things for them. In many cases people need to learn to do things for themselves. Our assistance should set people free rather than bind them.

5) "Can I permit him to be what he is? Can I allow him the freedom to be or to become what he is?" This is the difference between help that programs a person into what you think he should be and one that allows a person to discover his own program. The tendency to try and program is the trap we all fall into. The pathway seems so clear to us; we think that all we need to do is shove a little and the other person will be on his way. But this not only robs a person of discovery, it makes them dependent on the direction of others. There are always problems when we do this type of thing. Many people have been set up for failure by parents, teachers, and friends who select their pathways for them all their lives. In many cases, they choose failure for themselves rather than the success someone else has picked for them.

6) "Can I meet this other individual as a person who is in the process of becoming, or will I be bound by his past and my past?" For Christians, this means that we see each person as a part of God's creation, in the process of becoming what he's been created to be. We can be part of this exciting process, but we must leave the choices up to the person involved. We don't impose our direction, values, or choices on anyone.

When we share our lives with someone, that's what we do—we share our lives. No matter how good our lives or the things we are involved in might be, we can't, we shouldn't try to program that into the other person. We're responsible for our lives to God. Taking on the responsibility for another person's life just isn't realistic.

Of course I'm sad when my friends choose paths that

are not helpful for them, and I'm glad when they make choices that help them grow and develop. But I can't let my ego become involved in their success or failure. Often when I talk with parents about their troubled children, I become aware that the parents are really worried about their own self-concepts—"If my kids mess up, how will I look as a parent? I've failed." This is a heavy burden to carry. So parents try to make sure their children do just the right things, they try to program them so they won't make mistakes. But this eliminates their freedom as human beings and cripples their growth and development.

This also applies to the way some groups treat new Christians. One can tell certain groups of Christians by how they dress, talk, pray, wear their hair, vote, etc. They have been programed; someone has taken the responsibility for their choices, and therefore their lives. These groups tend to be very rigid; there's usually no place for confession or for differences. The result is lives that retain hidden, secret material, lives that are not open or free. It is difficult to grow in this type of situation.

People have great value. Each person is unique; he should be allowed to develop his own unique personality. He shouldn't be shoved, pushed, crowded, or molded. Jesus never did this. And as Christians we follow the example of Jesus. A person who is a servant should help others, not out of his or her own need to be a helpful person, but because of the motivation and experience of God's love. The sharing community can provide this type of person.

10.

COMMUNITY
AND
EVANGELISM

COMMUNITY AND EVANGELISM

"Men of Israel, I beg you to listen to my words. Jesus of Nazareth was a man proved to you by God himself through the works of power, the miracles and the signs which God showed through him here amongst you—as you very well know. . . . Now therefore the whole nation of Israel must know beyond the shadow of a doubt that this Jesus, whom you crucified, God has declared to be both Lord and Christ" (Acts 2:22, 36).

This was Peter's proclamation to the Jews who had witnessed the day of Pentecost in Jerusalem. He told about the life, death, and resurrection of Jesus; he explained the meaning of these events. This is what we call evangelism—the spreading of the "Good News." But there's something more to evangelism than this, and I think it's important that we look at it.

Peter's proclamation at Pentecost was the inevitable result of a changed life. Tradition tells us that when Peter was first called to be a "fisher" of men he was very young, barely out of his teens. A fisherman by trade, he probably had been brought up without the frills or fineries of life. I'm sure he had great difficulty expressing himself when he was in the company of men with better educations and more refined ways of life than his. When he first followed Jesus, Peter knew very little about

83

him; he had been taught about the Messiah in the temple, but he had trouble equating the Messiah with Jesus.

The Peter portrayed in Acts was a different person than he had been as a fisherman or even as a disciple. The Resurrection and the Holy Spirit had changed him. And his message that day was the product of that change, the product of an encounter with Jesus and the life in his community. Peter's words came out of his life experience. He was telling about his life, and what he had learned by living with Jesus. What a contrast to this same Peter denying he even knew the Lord on the night of Jesus' trial.

This is what evangelism means in the Christian community. It is the natural outgrowth of community, the process of witnessing to changes so dynamic they have to be shared. Many times we get caught up in the methodology of evangelism. I live in a section of the country where you can turn on the radio almost any time and be "evangelized." But much of what we hear is not evangelism; real evangelism is not a method. It is a shared experience of Christ, the Holy Spirit, and the Christian community. When these are not at the heart of evangelism, it fails, no matter what method is used.

Real evangelism involves offering people a viable alternative to the lives they're living. And people are looking for this kind of option. This is true of Barry. Barry had been coming to see me for quite a while; we had talked at length about his destructive lifestyle. Barry was using a lot of drugs. And this was surprising because his parents were involved with the church; as a matter of fact, his father was an elder.

Barry told me, "I've looked at Christianity for a long time. I went to church every Sunday until I came here to college. I really wish I could get into that, but it's hard. The people I know who claim to be Christian have the same attitudes and ideas that my non-Christian friends have. Some of my non-Christian friends are even better people. I don't really see that much difference in the Christians. "I really want to get into a different lifestyle, but what I've seen of Christianity, it's part of the same thing."

Barry's ideas about Christianity are not unique; I've heard similar comments many times. People like Barry are hungry for the kind of alternative lifestyle the Christian community can provide; they need to be confronted with the people whose lives have been changed because of their experience. This kind of evangelism is more than just talk, more than "evangelizing."

Some of the most important evangelism is accomplished on a one-to-one basis. What I mean is a life on a life— sharing. As we listen and talk, we delve into the issues that are most important to us. Eventually our relationship with Christ and our experiences in the Christian community come up. This is a very natural thing, not forced or preplanned. I don't have an outline of what I say; my sharing comes out of my life experiences. And because all of us have great spiritual needs, this sharing strikes a responsive note in people. They listen. Sometimes I don't share Christ with my friends for weeks or months after our introduction. Sometimes it happens on the first day. But when it does happen, we're both ready; the time has been spent getting the ground in shape.

Evangelism also involves the stimulation of growth and development in a person. This happened in the Christian community described in Acts. The older, more mature Christians would take the younger ones under their wing. The relationship was much like that of the older brother or sister in a family. They taught the younger ones, counseled them, and gave them a living example to pattern their lives after. The relationship between Paul and Timothy was like that.

This happens in our sharing community. Scooter was a new Christian with a rather limited background in the Bible and Christianity. He first became attracted to a young adult community because of some friends who shared their experiences with him. Scooter became involved in the community. After a year, he had grown more in knowledge of Christianity than had anyone else in the community. He read everything he could get his hands on—the Bible, books of theology, anything at all about Christianity. Every week the community met to study the Bible or discuss theology; usually one of the older Christians led the study. Frequently there was a book table supplied by the Intervarsity Christian Fellowship. The community, by providing an atmosphere of learning and study, helped in Scooter's growth.

Sometimes this nurturing kind of evangelism leads to more evangelism! Susan joined our community as a high school student, and later became part of our young adult community. Unlike Scooter, she came from a very religious background and knew quite a bit about the Bible. She was a very capable and valuable worker. But she had a hard time seeing this. I remember how fearful she was the first few times she went to the high school to meet students and share her life with them. "What will I say if they ask me a question I can't answer? I don't know what I'm doing; I really can't do this." As time went on, she found that she could share her life with others, that it wasn't all that bad if she could not answer a question. This was a time of real growth for her, a time of becoming what she was created to be. In the six years she was a member of the Christian community here, she grew in all phases of her life. She became the unique person she was meant to be; she discovered herself. Now she's in another city and another Christian community. She's also very much a part of the institutional church. Her days of growing, learning, discovering will go on a long time.

Evangelism is the natural outgrowth of a genuine Christian community. It can't be contained. It is contagious. This is the way God intended: people are evangelized, join the community, learn, grow, are taught, and then share their lives and experiences with others.

11.

THE
NONPOWER
MODEL

THE NONPOWER
MODEL

"I don't care if the doctor did order sleep therapy. We're not going to carry out his orders; it's not going to be done here." Sleep therapy had been ordered for a very disturbed patient on a psychiatric ward. But sleep therapy involves a great deal of nursing care, and the nurses didn't want to do it. This struggle went deeper than the specific treatment. It had to do with power and who had it: If the physician had it, his orders would be carried out; if the nurses had it, there would be no sleep therapy.

Some of the well-known citizens of our community have been caught gambling—an illegal offense. I know a young man who was caught selling marijuana and LSD; that's also against the law. Yet while my adult friends got off very lightly, my young friend may go to prison for five years or longer. Again, we're talking about power —some have it, some don't. And our society seems to be built on a structure of power. I go to the jails of our community for psychiatric evaluations. Most of the people there are young, or poor, or members of minority groups. They are people who lack power in a power-structured society.

A few weeks ago, I was sued by a patient. This happens quite frequently to physicians and I had paid little attention to this sort of thing before. But this time it was me. I felt absolutely powerless, vulnerable; I was in an acute state of anxiety. Now, I do have some power in society, and I was able to work out the situation quickly. But what if I had had no power at all? For the first time, perhaps, I felt what it was like to be powerless. Some people feel this way all the time and it doesn't feel good!

Many ask, "Why is there so much cheating and stealing in our society? Why is there so much dishonesty?" The basic answer to these questions centers around the reasons we do or don't do certain things. For instance, if I demand that my kids be honest in their dealings and not cheat or steal, yet get my tickets fixed or alter my income tax, I show them that right and wrong have nothing to do with morality but everything to do with power. As the adult male figure in the family, I have a lot of power; I can and do set the rules. If I'm not governed by these same rules, then the rules are equated with power, not morality. My kids will have no qualms about going against these rules; they may just worry about getting caught.

Society is a lot like this. Most of the people in jails are basically powerless people. If they are caught breaking the law, they go to jail. People in power who get caught have their hands slapped and go their way. There are many examples of this in our society. It says in a loud and clear voice things are up for the taking if you're strong enough or can get away with it. The poor, the blacks, and the young know this. They live in a society that "rips them off" constantly. Many of them have no problems taking what they can get their hands on.

Even our families are set up along power lines. Mary came to see me, worried about what was happening in her marriage: "Paul started out by being a little late for supper. He then got to the point of not coming home until eight o'clock. For the past six weeks, he has not come home until ten or eleven. I don't understand what's going on." Paul's answer was, "I just don't feel comfortable in my living room. There isn't a chair I can sit in. I don't really know why I don't come home, but I guess it has to do with feeling uncomfortable." Paul was making a power play; his actions were saying, "You do this to me and I'll get you back by doing something else; you control the home and shut me out, and I'll not come home."

Mankind's preoccupation with power is very old. Even Jesus' disciples were concerned with it; they asked, "Who is really greatest in the kingdom of Heaven?" But Jesus made it clear that his kingdom was to be different. He picked up a little child and said, "Unless you change your whole outlook and become like little children, you will never enter the kingdom of Heaven. It is the man who can be as humble as this little child who is greatest in the kingdom of Heaven" (Matt. 18:1–4). This isn't an isolated passage of scripture; this concept permeates the gospels. The Christian way of relating is diametrically opposed to the power structure of the world.

Now if the nonpower model is the Christian way of relating to people, how does it work? In the sharing community, it means that we look at our brothers and sisters in Christ as unique products of God's creation, and make it our task to help these people grow and develop into the persons they were meant to be. We avoid the tendency to take control of the group, to try to program others and make them conform to the group model. And we confront any members of the group we see trying to take this kind of control.

"This may work in a Christian community, but it sure doesn't sound like a good idea in my dog-eat-dog world.

I have to compete to even stay afloat." In the nitty-gritty of life, it's difficult to live out the Christian lifestyle of humility. It's difficult not to exercise power when we have it. But this is at the heart of the question—what do we do with the power we have? Do we use it as a club to keep ourselves at the top of the heap? Or do we allow others to share in this power? Do we give power to the powerless?

I have had the opportunity to see how the nonpower model can function in an actual working situation. As the psychiatrist on an inpatient ward, I have a good deal of power; I can write orders and most of the time have them carried out. But if this ward is to be run on a nonpower basis, others have to be involved in decisions. This is what has happened. There are nurses, social workers, and attendants on the ward. Each person has input into the decision-making process. This doesn't mean everyone has equal votes in areas he or she is not trained in; for instance, I listen carefully to everyone's opinion on patient medication but I do not jeopardize the health or safety of patients by using medication in a dangerous way. But I have seen that the more people have input into these kinds of decisions, the more they learn, and the more they learn, the more valuable their contribution is. This process works for all of us; by having input into decisions about social work and nursing care, I have learned things I had never known before!

Sometimes there are problems with running a psychiatric ward in this manner. Some people are so accustomed to being in control that they try to take over whenever the opportunity arises. Some people just can't grasp the nonpower system. When this happens, our ward staff usually handles the situation by direct confrontation. They are kind but firm in demanding that control and power-grabbing are not tolerated. Some people have left because of this; others have learned to exist with the system.

The results of our nonpower system have been very interesting. Our unit functions as a community. The members of the staff work together. The relationships between the community members are quite good, and morale is high. Staffers are actively involved with patients rather than fighting each other for control; this in turn benefits the patients. The Psych Unit has become a fun place to work, a place where people have discovered some of their unique gifts. It's a place where people care about each other; for one person, at least, the people affiliated with the ward are family.

Now, I can only talk about my experiences on the psychiatric unit. I don't know how this would work in an insurance or law office, or a big-business operation. I know that when the business community is involved, someone has to make decisions. But I also know that in offices where people are involved in decision-making, where they are made to feel important, morale is higher and, I would imagine, productivity greater.

It would be foolish for me to deny the existence of power and its importance to society. Power is all around us; the Christian, as well as the non-Christian, has it. As a matter of fact, I myself have a lot of power; I shudder to think that I have the power to influence a judge to send a person to a state mental hospital. So the issue is: how do we use our power? Do we try to gain our own selfish objectives with it?

What happens when we're in a power struggle with someone else? Do we allow ourselves to be run over? This is a hard question, and one that demands individual consideration. If I had allowed powerful people to take over the psychiatric ward, its purpose as a nonpower structure would have been thwarted. It takes power to prevent the powerful from grabbing power, and power to give it to the powerless. We can't deny the existence or even the need for power, but we can use real care in what we do with it; we can examine our motives and our ego involvement with it.

As Christians, our morality—our sense of right or wrong—should have as little to do with power as possible. It should deal with what is just and right. This puts me in an awkward position from time to time. I'm opposed to violence and to people ripping each other off. At times I find myself at great odds with the laws of our land and the people in power. They don't dictate my code of ethics or my morality. This can be costly to me professionally and personally.

At other times, I'm at odds with the powerless and disenfranchised. The fact that they have been wronged doesn't justify their doing the same or taking part in violence. Our standards of right and wrong must be rooted in morality and justice or we will lose our sense of moral values and we will set ourselves up for gigantic struggles for power and control, with little regard to what's just or fair.

The issue of power, then, boils down to some basic choices for me. I have power as a psychiatrist, as a parent, and as a husband. My whiteness means power. So does my income. The big question is, do I use it, or do I share it? Do I give it away? Our society is based on a power structure which permeates our jobs, our schools, our churches—even our families. I have to live in the structure, but I can still control my end of things.

Specifically, this means I can learn to give up some of the power I have. Now, I like power; I like the security of having power. But if my wife, children, and the people I work with and pray with are to grow and develop into what they're meant to be, I've got to let them. I've got to be part of an environment that will allow them to discover themselves. This means that we're not into a power struggle in which we put each other down to gain control. Instead, we are helping each other grow and develop into the unique persons God created us to be. This is what the Christian community should be all about —the discovery and the development of people, so that all of us grow. The opposite of the power-based society; this is uniquely Christian.

12.

STARTING A SHARING COMMUNITY

STARTING A SHARING
COMMUNITY

One of the unique things about the communities in Acts is that they just appeared. The needed ingredients were there—people committed to the risen Lord and to each other, the Holy Spirit to draw them together, the houses for them to meet in. These needed ingredients are still present today—what we need to do is rediscover them. Christian community is here. The task for us is to discover and implement it, to find out where it is and to activate it.

Many of our churches want desperately to be God's community. Some succeed, but many don't. Many have some aspects of Christian community. But it's very difficult to feel part of a Christian community in a big room with five hundred to a thousand people we hardly know, although this type of corporate worship is part of the function of the Christian community.

So how does community start? In a very simple way, with one person (you or me) and the conviction that Christian community is a biblical concept, necessary for growth, development, and even survival as a Christian. This is a starting point. What we need now is someone else—perhaps a husband or a wife—who shares this conviction.

One of the best community experiences I ever had involved only one other person and the sharing of our individual lives. As time went on, we interested more people; our wives became part of the process; other couples joined us. Before long, so many people had wanted to join that we were in danger of becoming too large. Growth depends on contact with others who are interested in getting involved with community. They are around. Pray that God will direct you together.

Once this special person is found, the next step is to pray together about Christian community, to begin to share lives. A study of the Scriptures will reveal that God has much to say about Christian community. The Old Testament is rich in the concept of community; the children of Israel were God's community in a very real sense. The Book of Acts, Paul's writings, and the Gospels are filled with ideas about Christian community. When I read these books with the idea of Christianity in mind, I'm amazed at how much they have to say!

It is important to decide on a time to meet together regularly. Because the process of sharing takes time, anything under one hour is unrealistic. Start meeting regularly right away! How frequently these meetings take place depends on you, but once a week is reasonable.

If there are only two of you, it is easier to get started sharing; the atmosphere will be more relaxed and questions can be asked and answered with less strain. If the group is large, breaking the ice is more of a problem. A good way to get acquainted is to have each person share something about his or her childhood—where he or she was born and grew up, special experiences, whatever is meaningful to the individual. Early experiences have a profound influence on us; sharing them can reveal a great deal. Revealing a past experience is also relatively safe; it's a nonthreatening way to begin the process of sharing. This process of getting acquainted may go on for two or three weeks. The group will spend a lot of time just milling around, not getting into anything profound. But this is the way trust begins.

Another good way to start a group is to read a book and discuss it; that is how the group I'm presently involved in began. A Bible study could also be the center of sharing. Setting aside time for prayer is a natural opening for sharing. All of us have needs, and things we are praying about; we pray about things that are meaningful and important to us. Taking time for everyone to share requests is a good way to get to know each other. Friendship deepens through shared concerns.

Along the way a format has to be worked out. I have found it is best to keep this simple. It could center around time spent in Bible study, sharing, and praying together. In our community we solved the leadership problem by revolving the leadership responsibilities from week to week according to where we were meeting; the couple who hosted the group provided the leadership. This plan insured against one person taking control of the group, and provided for everyone in the group being ministered to equally. These are just suggestions; there are other formats and leadership possibilities. The format and organization of the group really aren't that important. The important thing is to establish an atmosphere for meaningful sharing between members of the group.

How does a person share his life with another human being? Let me say right off—with real difficulty. For most of us this process is scary; we don't want to share ourselves; we don't know how to begin. We all have many images of ourselves; we show one side of ourselves at work, another at home, still another at church. One side of ourselves is for show; the other we keep hidden. And much of our public self is a cover-up. We wish to create the image that we are problem-free, unruffled, "together," although this might not be the case with our private selves at all. We're hesitant to reveal our imperfect selves. Trust must develop before we show this side of ourselves to the group, before we begin to share our whole selves.

The development of trust in the group is a slow process. It is helped by the early "get-acquainted" sessions. Sooner or later someone will test the group by revealing something of themselves, usually a past experience or feeling that has lost some of its emotional charge. If the group deals with this in a constructive, helpful way, the way will be opened for individuals to share things that have a greater emotional charge.

After our group had been together for a few meetings, Jane said to Francis, "You always seem to think you know it all. I'm tired of your thinking you're right all the time. You never listen to the rest of us." After that, silence. Wow! Where do we go from there? This is a rather common occurrence in groups. Negative feelings are expressed to test the group's ability to handle this kind of thing. The individual wonders: Is this a safe place to expose myself? Will I be cut down or listened to? What type of reaction will this bring? If the group can pass this test, trust grows.

After the group has been tested in many ways, after trust has been developed, someone in the group eventually will reveal himself in a very personal way. A few meetings after Jane's outburst, Sam related, "As a Christian, I'm supposed to be a perfect father and husband. I find, though, that I fail in these areas many times. I'm supposed to be a leader, so I pretend that I don't fail. I live behind a big wall." When someone pulls off a mask like that, the group can move to a deeper level. It stays at that level for a while, then moves deeper as other members of the group share themselves.

How much of himself should a person share in a sharing community? Not everything—there are parts of everyone that belong only to him or her and are known only by God. We all have a right to a private world; that's a special place for us. There's nothing wrong with hanging on to it, as long as it doesn't keep us from sharing those parts of our lives we *can* share. Absolute openness is like absolute honesty. Both are good concepts, but must have limitations. I must admit, however, that those parts of me I keep to myself are becoming smaller and smaller as I become more involved in community.

What to share depends on the individual. I look into various aspects of my life and share them. For a long time, my work was problematical, so I just related what was going on at work. Since my work involves people, I shared my frustrations about some of the people I contacted on a day-to-day basis. This eased my frustrations and gave me a chance to get things off my chest, to acknowledge some of my feelings. As a result, I didn't take out as many of my frustrations on my family.

It's especially hard for me to share some of the things I'm going through at any particular moment; I tend to wait until I'm through a struggle before I talk about it in my group. I'm learning, however, that there are real rewards of support, trust, love, and concern if I share some of my current life situations with my community.

One night someone in the group brought up the fact that no one ever really talked about their marriages. This is a touchy area for sharing in community. I can talk about my working situations because no one who works with me is in the group; I'm not going to be challenged. But my wife *is* in the group; she's there to challenge me or give her side of issues. So we planned one night to talk about our family relationships. The men and women met separately on this night; this freed some of us to the extent that we were enabled to share. And we broke down some barriers that night. We had to come to grips with the fact that our marriages and families aren't perfect, and there are some things in these areas we need to share.

One thing we don't do enough of in the Christian community is to share our dreams and aspirations. Often we are so wrapped up in everyday life that we hardly think of them. But many times dreams come true, and sharing them with others helps. Some of my dreams have been implemented by the community, many have been encouraged, some have even been discouraged. At times I feel like letting myself go and dreaming the most impossible dreams I can think of. Out of our wildest dreams, sometimes, come the greatest things. If I dare to dream and share and perhaps look foolish, perhaps others of my community will dare to dream also.

The process of sharing, of building trust, continues as long as the group exists. The more the process goes on, the more feedback we get about how we appear to others. We learn that we don't always have to be the "nice guy." We can express our feelings and failures and still be accepted. At times, there will be direct confrontation: "I think you and John are very rude. You didn't even allow Frank to lead the discussion or do anything he wanted to do and it's his house and his turn to lead. You're just selfish!" This was shouted out with great emotion in one of our group meetings, and it was true. The community can tolerate this kind of confrontation and survive.

"I would never have picked any of you for my friends." These are things you don't really say to people. But when trust develops, you can. Negative feelings as well as positive ones can be expressed. A basic honesty develops. When a group has gotten this far, the members accept each other and feel accepted. What each feels as part of the community is, in a real sense, the foundation for his or her own self-acceptance. We know God accepts us through Christ. Now we become aware that these people right here accept us. This makes it easier to accept ourselves. And with this process begins change.

The community is a place for expression of positive as well as negative feelings: "I really like you. You're a very warm and generous person. I knew this the very first time we met." Positive interpersonal feelings are expressed in the group. This builds trust. Also present in the group are many warm, loving encounters. This is truly a time of agape. The love of God is literally experienced between the brothers and sisters of the community. I could honestly say to my community after a year of meeting together, "I wouldn't have picked any of you for friends, let alone someone to share my life with, yet I love you all in a deep, significant way and would do anything for you."

There will be times when everyone in the community just sits there, when the meeting is open for sharing and no one shares. No one feels like it, or there's nothing to share. Everyone's anxious and tense—now what? Well, that's one of the things we have to learn to put up with in a group. If we can get over the anxiety of these silent periods, they can be meaningful experiences; they help us learn the difference between allowing things to happen and trying to program them. As time goes on, these silent periods become more tolerable.

Sharing is not the only function of the Christian community; Bible study and prayer also play important parts. The subject of study may be chosen by the couple hosting the meeting in their home, or chosen by the group in advance. Prayer develops out of sharing personal needs; we pray for persons outside the group as well as group members.

As more people become interested in the group, the problem of limiting the group may come up. We limited our community to twelve; we just can't handle any more people. At times, even this small a group can become impersonal, so we divide the group into three groups of four. The complexion of the group depends on the people who make it up and the changes that they're going through. New people alter this process, and it's difficult to develop trust when the group changes all the time. The other side of the coin, of course, is the danger of becoming elitist or snobbish. We try to avoid this problem by helping others get started with their groups. We also open the group to others for a communion service or other special occasions. Our group, however, is uniquely ours; this is an important concept for us.

The sharing community will not always move forward at the same pace. Sometimes it will even seem that the group is moving backward. There may be long periods when nothing significant is shared. At times the group is stagnant and frustrating. At other times, there is so much negative feedback that the whole process seems destructive. And sometimes even the forward progress is maddeningly slow and plodding. The giant steps forward are unusual. But all this is part of the group process.

This is a look at how a Christian community develops. It's centered in and through Jesus Christ and the Holy Spirit. It's composed of people who love him and each other. They spend time getting to know each other, often discussing superficial subjects. Eventually negative feelings are expressed, as the group is tested and trust develops.

People tell how they feel about each other. Acceptance grows, both in the group and in the individual members. Members learn to share; the masks (or part of them) come down; private selves are exposed. The group moves into deeper interpersonal relationships. People learn to look at themselves, learn to admit who they are, and to get involved in the process of becoming who they were created to be.

13.

WHAT CAN WE BRING TO COMMUNITY?

WHAT CAN WE BRING TO COMMUNITY?

Each member of the Christian community is important. Each person has a contribution to make. And the progress of the group depends on the attitudes and commitments each person brings with him to the community.

It goes without saying that each person must bring to the community a spiritual awareness and interest centered in Jesus Christ, an *openness* to the possibility of a spiritual life involving a relationship with Christ and relationships with others in the community. Our group ranged from members committed to Christ in a personal relationship to those with a great interest in Christianity and a willingness to discover what it is all about to those very skeptical about the validity of the Christian faith but willing to be active participants in the group. It is imperative that some members of the group be involved in a relationship with Christ and know to some extent what this relationship is like.

Along with an openness to the possibility of a spiritual life there must be an openness to the concept of personal growth and change. This is especially important for members who have been involved in the Christian experience for a long time. It's hard to grow and develop when we feel comfortable. There is a human tendency for the long-time Christian to feel he or she has become an expert with all the answers, to see no reason for change. We forget that the Christian life is not static; it's a life of growth and development and discovery. One of my first reactions to my group was "how can I learn from these people? I've been a Christian almost as long as some of them have been alive." I forgot how unique each of God's creatures is, and what we can learn from each other. I learned that length of time sometimes has nothing to do with spiritual growth, and that some of my new friends who had known Christ only a short time were farther down the road in certain areas of their spiritual growth and development than I was.

Each member of the community must bring the attitude of *trust* into this community. Every person must trust the group to set its own course, chart its own direction. The alternative to this is a group that has its direction set before it begins. I have to struggle with this every time I become involved in a new group. I remember past experiences and want to relive them. So I try to direct the group in a specific way. There is within me a strong desire to be the "leader." But if I let this happen, the group can go only in the direction I want it. This is unfair to the others in the community, and it leaves out the Holy Spirit as the director and leader of the group. The goals of the group must be a composite of the group's needs, and be in a process of change as the group changes. Certainly one broad goal is for all members of the group to grow and develop as Christians within the Christian community. The specific goals will vary according to the group. But since they are a composite of all the members, they will probably differ from every other group any of the members has been involved in before.

It is vital that each person come to the group as a participant. Community means *involvement*. This means every member brings his or her whole person—ideas as

114

well as feelings—to the group. No one can hold back and be an observer. Now it's easy to say this, but hard to do. At times, I feel I just can't participate; at other times, I participate too much, to the extent that I crowd other people out of their chance to participate. No person brings perfection to the group, but each can bring an attitude of involvement.

The hardest times for me to be a participator is when I'm going through a trying experience—when I'm down or when things just aren't going right. My first inclination is to withdraw and not get involved. But these times are when I need community the most! If I can break through the barrier and share my feelings, the community comes forward and meets my needs. But they can't help me if I don't show myself. At these times I must make the extra effort at involvement and communication.

Another attitude the individual member must bring to the group is *acceptance*. I remember walking into a community meeting once, and seeing a couple I had heard about but not met. I had not liked what I heard, so I was not overjoyed when I was told they were to be part of our group. When they spied me for the first time I could tell I wasn't alone in my feelings. Here was a barrier I had to surmount. But barriers like these are assets, not liabilities. They provide room for growth and development. In the two years we've met together something has happened. The other night the woman of the couple leaned over to me and said, "I love you, and that's really saying something." I knew what she meant; I loved her also. We had learned to accept each other. And it took time, but it was necessary if we were ever to become a community.

Listening is crucial in the Christian community. Some nights I just don't feel like it; I don't care what the other person is sharing and I'm not interested in what he's trying to communicate. I am in my own world, thinking about home, or the hospital, or something else. Thank goodness there are others at these times who *are* interested and who show empathetic understanding, because I have been listened to in this way and know how much it can help. One night in our group meeting I expressed great concern over the establishment of an adolescent halfway house in our hometown. The next night we were to have a meeting at my house to discuss the project. Every person from our group showed up at the meeting and supported me. They had listened with empathetic understanding to my concern!

What can the individual bring to the group? He or she can bring some attitudes that help the community—openness, trust, involvement, acceptance, listening. Each person must struggle to make his or her behavior approach these attitudes. None of us has arrived as a mature Christian yet; as Keith Miller puts it, we are all in the process of becoming.

What we do when we come to the community is bring ourselves. We come as persons. And we need to deal with the personal in others. Sometimes this presents a problem, but it also provides room for growth. And growth is really what the community is all about.

14.

WHAT MY COMMUNITY IS LIKE

WHAT MY COMMUNITY
IS LIKE

The community I am presently involved in began out
of a program of events on Sunday. I was asked to lead a
discussion group at our church based on Keith Miller's
great book, *The Taste of New Wine*. The discussion was
to extend for six weeks. During that time, we began sharing our lives with each other, and by the sixth week some
of us wanted to continue meeting. Four couples decided to
meet in homes, going from house to house once a week
for another six weeks. When this time had passed, the
group again elected to continue. By the time eighteen
weeks had gone by, two couples had been added to the
group and we just kept going.

The basis for our group was our common belief in
Jesus Christ. When we started, we were involved in
various stages of belief and commitment. One couple had
been involved in the institutional church for quite some
time and had had no exposure to anything outside this
affiliation. Another couple had recently experienced the
joy of a new relationship with Christ and had experienced
some special and wonderful gifts of the Holy Spirit. Their
newfound joy permeated everything they did. Still another couple had been in a denominational church that
really "turned them on." They had had a taste of Christian community and wanted more. In still another case,
the wife was an involved Christian with joy and enthusi-

asm; her husband was interested but wanted to evaluate the situation. The fifth couple was highly committed and involved in the institutional church; the last couple had become Christians before they were married and had been active in churches and community then. As you can see, although we were united in Christ, we came from different backgrounds and were at different stages in our Christian growth and development. Our backgrounds also differed in regard to Biblical knowledge and theology.

Our differences did not stop there. Some of us were in our thirties, some forties, some fifties. Politically we thought and voted differently. We came from different occupations. Although we all had children, our families were of different ages and stages of development. Some of the wives worked, some didn't. I would not have picked very many from the group for close friends; I certainly wouldn't have picked many to share my life with. Yet these people have stretched me in many directions and I had to deal with emotions and ideas I normally would have let go by the board because of my own prejudices. The differences between the people that make up the group is one of its strong points.

With these differences, it is easy to see that this group has some unique qualities. It is important to realize this because it is a natural tendency to want to program our communities according to our past group experiences or our ideas of what community should be. If we allow this to happen, we are sure to be disappointed, because each group is unique. We cannot get hung up looking for what went on in the past. This is a *new* experience, with new people. Community must be a time of discovery; this means allowing things to happen as the Holy Spirit moves among us and we get to know each other. If a group is forced to follow preconceived lines or previous experi-

ences, much of its discovery and uniqueness will be lost.
Our format is rather simple. We decided very early
that we didn't want a leader. Often leaders minister but
are not ministered to; we didn't want this to happen. So
we decided that the couple who hosted the week's meeting would plan the program and serve as leaders. As a
result of this rotating leadership there is a lot of variety in
what we do. Sometimes we study scripture; at other times
we talk about world events in the light of a Biblical per-
spective. Sometimes we study the Sunday lesson in advance; this makes the Sunday worship service much more
meaningful to all of us. Another advantage of our rotating
system is that many of us have discovered leadership
capabilities we never knew we had!

Included in the format every week is the opportunity
for sharing our lives with the other people in the community. At times this never gets off the ground. At other
times it is a very meaningful experience. Some people
share and others listen, support, encourage, and help. It is
during these times that we learn to love and care for each
other, when we learn to say, "I can't make it on my own,
I need your help." During these times I can take off some
of my masks and remove some barriers.

It was and still is hard for many of us in the group to
open up and reveal what was happening to us on a personal level. There are some things we could not share and
still can't. But as trust has developed among the members
of the group, many small advances have been made. There
have been no real astounding breakthroughs, but people
have moved gradually into the process of sharing.

We have experienced periods of time in which very little is shared. These are frustrating, but we have learned
that they are part of the process. We allow people to be
themselves. No one is forced to share. It has been our

experience that things will eventually start moving again.

After sharing and study, we always spend time praying for each other. At first we stood in a circle and held hands. Later we sat on the floor. As time went on, we found that we were praying for longer periods of time and beginning to call each other during the week for prayer when our lives were troubled.

We began to get together outside the meetings for other reasons, too. On occasions we gather for parties or meals. Some of the couples spend their leisure time together. We have become friends; the group plays an increasingly important role in our lives.

This doesn't mean the group process is always pleasant, or always easy. Growing and developing is never an easy task; often it is painful and frustrating. At times, all of us have wanted to quit. But the thing that keeps us coming back is the effect the community has on our lives. We may disagree in many areas, but we all agree that the community has changed us. I hear this over and over from members of the group:

I have a hard time with direct confrontation but I've learned to live with it and benefit from it. I feel that because of this experience, I've grown and developed in many areas of my life . . .

When I came into the community, I wasn't sure about God or Christ and now I'm committed to him. This came about through our study of the scriptures and the discussions that followed. . . . I haven't always agreed with everything that was said . . . on more than one occasion I left the meeting very angry, but it made me think . . .

I discovered that I could really do something, that I had some gifts and talents. This has helped me look at myself in a new light. . . . I'm also in greater touch with my feelings; I don't feel as bad after I'm angry. . . . This has come about because of the affirmation and love that I feel in the community . . .

I'm not as comfortable in my suburban home as I once was. . . . Things have lost some of their value for me and I'm being forced to struggle and rethink my whole position on materialism. Some of the things I've studied in the scripture have made me uncomfortable in this area . . .

My attitude towards people has really changed. I can love a person even though he has a different point of view than mine. I've learned to respect another way of looking at things . . .

The group for me has been a struggle. . . . I'm still frustrated, at times, with our lack of movement. . . . If I take things one week at a time, I find I'm standing still. When I look at things over over a six-month period, I find we've made real progress . . .

I'm finally beginning to grasp what Paul said when he warned us not to let the world shove us into its mold. I used to think this had to do with a list of things I called "worldly." This isn't it at all. It has to do with the world's standards and what's considered normal. This has been a big challenge to my own Christian existence. . . . When you get down to it, we're all nice and dishonest. The community is taking out some of my "niceness" and I'm dealing more with the reality of life. I'm not as nice as I used to be, but I'm more honest with myself and others . . .

Community for me has meant being in a process of changing my life. . . . I wouldn't go back to the old me for anything, even though at times I fail and have setbacks. I've been involved with the church for a long time and intend to continue my involvement. My sharing community doesn't take away from this, it adds to it. I feel more a part of the church than I ever did . . .

These people have all experienced community. For them it has been a revolutionary force in their lives. It's brought about many profound changes and has shaken the foundations of their beings. They're changing, struggling, growing people. They're people who are trying to walk the way they talk. This has been hard for them, yet none of them would go back to the old way. This experience has brought new meaning to their lives. They've had a renewed experience with the living God and this has had a deep effect on them.

I am one of these people, one of those involved in the process of becoming the persons God created them to be. This process will go on until we are involved in God's final transformation. Until that time, I am committed to community. If I stay in the same city, it will be the community I'm presently involved in. If I move, I will find another one or attempt to bring one together. It's mandatory for me as a Christian to be in community with God's people, people who are willing to share their lives and share in the process of Christian growth and development.

BIBLIOGRAPHY

Bonhoeffer, Dietrich. *The Cost of Discipleship*. New York: MacMillan, Inc., 1967.

——. *Life Together*. New York: Harper & Row, 1976.

Erikson, Erik H. *Childhood and Society*. New York: W. W. Norton, 1964.

Jordan, Clarence. *The Cotton Patch Version of Hebrews and the General Epistles*. New York: Association Press, 1973.

——. *The Cotton Patch Version of Luke and Acts*. New York: Association Press, 1969.

——. *The Cotton Patch Version of Matthew and John*. New York: Association Press, 1970.

——. *The Cotton Patch Version of Paul's Epistles*. New York: Association Press, 1968.

——. *The Sermon on the Mount*. Valley Forge, PA: Judson Press, 1970.

Larson, Bruce. *Ask Me to Dance*. Waco, TX: Word Books, 1972.

——. *Dare to Live Now*. Waco, TX: Word Books, 1967.

——. *The Meaning and Mystery of Being Human*. Waco, TX: Word Books, 1978.

——. *No Longer Strangers*. Waco, TX: Word Books, 1971.

——. *The Relational Revolution*. Waco, TX: Word Books, 1976.

Miller, Keith. *The Becomers*. Waco, TX: Word Books, 1973.

——. *Habitation of Dragons*. Waco, TX: Word Books, 1970.

Miller, Keith. *Please Love Me.* Waco, TX: Word Books, 1977.

———. *A Second Touch.* Waco, TX: Word Books, 1967.

———. *A Taste of New Wine.* Waco, TX: Word Books, 1965.

Rogers, Carl. *On Becoming a Person.* Boston: Houghton Mifflin, 1970.

———. *On Encounter Groups.* New York: Harper & Row, 1973.

———. *Freedom to Learn: A View of What Education Might Become.* Columbus, OH: Charles E. Merrill, 1969.

Tournier, Paul. *Guilt and Grace.* New York: Harper & Row, 1962.

———. *The Meaning of Persons.* New York: Harper & Row, 1957.

———. *A Place for You.* New York: Harper & Row, 1968.